SPORTS THROUGHOUT HISTORY™

The History of
FOOTBALL

Diana Star Helmer and Thomas S. Owens

The Rosen Publishing Group's
PowerKids Press™
New York

Published in 2000 by The Rosen Publishing Group, Inc.
29 East 21st Street, New York, NY 10010

First Edition

Book Design: Michael de Guzman

Photo Credits: p. 4 © Paris Match/Archive Photos; p. 7 © Christophe Ena/AP Wide World Photos; p. 8 CORBIS/BETTMANN; p. 11 © Charlie Neibergall/AP Wide World Photos; pp. 12, 20 AP Wide World Photos; p. 15 © Archive Photos; p. 16 © Reuters/Mike Segar/Archive Photos; p. 18 CORBIS/BETTMANN-UPI.

Helmer, Diana Star, 1962-
      The history of football / by Diana Star Helmer and Thomas S. Owens.
           p.   cm.—(Sports throughout history)
      Includes index.
      Summary: Details the development of football throughout history, discussing improvements in the rules and equipment and the formation of related organizations.
      ISBN 0-8239-5471-4
      1. Football—History—Juvenile literature.   [1. Football—History.] I. Owens, Tom, 1960- . II. Title. III. Series: Helmer, Diana Star, 1962- Sports throughout history
GV950.H45 1999
796.33'09—dc21   98-56025
                                                                                      CIP
                                                                                      AC

Manufactured in the United States of America

Contents

Carried Away

Football is one of the most popular sports in the U.S. today, but it was not always played as it is now. Football's history began with the game of soccer. In soccer, players are not allowed to touch the ball with their hands. In 1823, a soccer player at Rugby School in England picked up the ball and carried it during a game. Both teams kept playing. It was fun, but it wasn't soccer. By changing the rules, the players had invented a new game. They named it after their school: rugby.

◀ *This ball is from a rugby game played in 1851. The oval ball was invented because it was easier to carry than a round one.*

A Whole New Ball Game

Just as rugby came from soccer, football came from rugby. In 1874, the Canadian McGill University rugby team taught Harvard University students to play rugby. Then, Harvard began playing a game with rules that were like rugby's. Harvard played its new game with other college teams in the United States. In 1876, athletes from some of those schools met to make sure that everyone would follow the same rules for the new game. They called their game football.

Rugby is played with an oval ball. Carrying the ball and tackling players is allowed. Harvard students liked playing this way and used these rules for football.

New Rules

A man named Walter Camp made some of football's longest-lasting rules. In the 1880s, he invented **downs**, which helped make sure that one team couldn't have the ball for the whole game. Camp also allowed **tackling** from shoulders to knees. Football got rougher. In 1905, many players were hurt during games. Eighteen were killed. President Theodore Roosevelt wanted to outlaw football because it was so dangerous. Instead, schools created better rules to make football safe.

◀ *Before Walter Camp changed the rule to allow tackling from shoulders to knees, players were only allowed to tackle from the waist up.*

Planning for Play

One new rule to make football safer let players throw the ball. Another had players from each team line up at a place on the field called the **line of scrimmage** at the beginning of each down. Spreading players out kept the person who had the ball from being tackled by too many people at once.

New rules gave teams new ways to surprise **opponents**. When a game plan worked, that **play** was used again. Knowing different plays helped teams win.

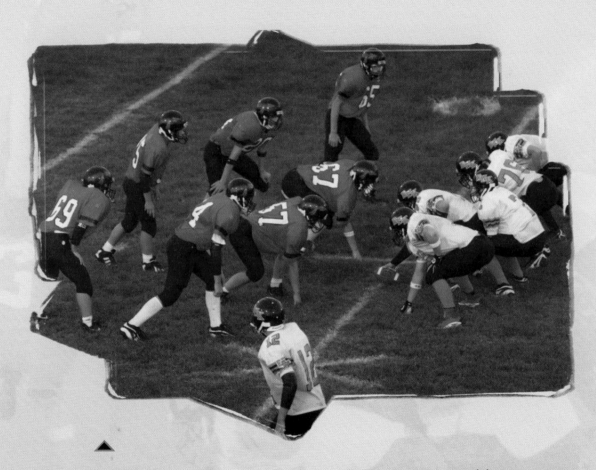

Once teams started to use game plans, players couldn't just play rough anymore. They had to study to learn the plays.

Taking Turns

Early football players often stayed on the field for a whole 60-minute game. The same player tried to score, then tried to stop the opponent. In 1941, a new rule said that coaches could change players as often as they wanted during games. This meant that players could become skillful in either **offense** or **defense**. Having players who were especially good at different jobs meant that teams played even better. Today, all college and **professional** football teams play this way.

◀ *After four downs, the coach has a chance to put the offense players or defense players out on the field.*

Seeing Stars

As far back as the 1890s, towns in the United States had professional football teams. Fans liked college teams better, though. Players stayed with the same team for their four years of college, so fans got to know and love them.

In 1925, professional football started to become more popular. A player named Red Grange finished college and joined the Chicago Bears. Thousands of people came to professional games just to see him.

Red Grange was called the "Galloping Ghost." He is said to be the player who got fans interested in professional football. ▶

The NFL

In 1920, professional teams formed the National Football League. Since fans wanted to see college stars, the NFL started the college draft in 1936. The draft let NFL teams take turns picking college players. In 1960, the new American Football League tried to hire all the best players away from the NFL. The two **leagues** fought until 1966, when they decided to join together. Now, all professional teams are in one of two divisions, or groups, that are part of the NFL.

◀ *The two NFL divisions are the National Football Conference and the American Football Conference. The best team from each division competes in the championship game.*

Simply Super

In 1966, the NFL **championship** game didn't have an official name. The owner of the Kansas City Chiefs, Lamar Hunt, named it the Super Bowl. The Green Bay Packers won the NFL's first Super Bowl in January 1967. A 1968 Super Bowl play-off game was also famous. It was so cold in Wisconsin, where the game was being played, that the field had to be kept under a cover and heated. The cover was taken off during the game, and the ground froze. Fans called it the "Ice Bowl."

Lamar Hunt got the name for the Super Bowl when he saw his daughter bouncing a ball called a Superball. Mr. Hunt's team, the Chiefs, lost the first Super Bowl to the Packers.

Football for Kids

In 1929, the Philadelphia YMCA started a football program for kids. Both girls and boys were allowed to play in these games, called "Pee-Wee" football. Kids played against other kids who were the same age and size. Only students who were doing well in school could play. The program was later named after a winning college coach, Pop Warner. Today, thousands of boys and girls play "Pop Warner" football in 39 states, Mexico, and Japan. Every player plays every game.

◄ *Kids who play "Pop Warner" football know that having fun on the field and getting good grades in school are as important as winning.*

21

Part of the family

In the U.S., many families spend time together watching football on TV. Football is often a part of Thanksgiving, Christmas, and other family holidays. People don't just watch football, they also play it in parks and backyards. Football has changed over the years, but it still brings fun and excitement to the people who love it.

Web Sites:

Check out this Web site on football: http://www.nfl.com

Glossary

championship (CHAM-pee-un-ship) The last game of a sports season that decides which team is the best.

defense (DEE-fents) When a team tries to stop the other team from scoring.

down (DOWN) One of four chances a football team has to go forward ten yards toward the goal line.

league (LEEG) A group of teams that play against each other in the same sport.

line of scrimmage (LYN UV SKRIH-mij) The imaginary line between two football teams as they face each other to begin a new play.

offense (AW-fents) When a team tries to score.

opponent (uh-POH-nint) The person or team you are playing against in a game.

play (PLAY) A move or series of moves in a game.

professional (pruh-FEH-shuh-nul) An athlete who earns money for playing a sport.

tackling (TA-kuh-ling) To stop an opponent by knocking him down.

Index